the brother swimming beneath me

Black Lawrence Press
www.blacklawrence.com

Executive Editor and Art Director: Colleen Ryor
Managing Editor: Diane Goettel
Book Design: Steven Seighman and Colleen Ryor

Black Lawrence Press
8405 Bay Parkway C8
Brooklyn, N.Y. 11214
U.S.A.

Published 2009 by Black Lawrence Press, a division of Dzanc Books

First edition 2009

Printed in the United States

the
brother
swimming
beneath me

poems by Brent Goodman

Black Lawrence Press
New York

contents

III : Spiral Course

Thanks to the editors of the following publications, where the following poems originally appeared, often in earlier versions:

The Adirondack Review - "Doors and Windows for a Room," "Wisconsin Triptych"
Anti- - "Information Age"
Barn Owl Review - "Lice"
The Beloit Poetry Journal - a selection from "Maier" (originally titled "Yom Kippur, 1979")
Court Green - "First Queer Poem"
Diagram - "Science Fiction"
Diode - "Cicada," "Cover, " Kodachrome Slides of my Father in Vietnam," "Recipe"
Green Mountains Review - "Moving Past"
Knockout - "Mayfly"
Limp Wrist - "By Definition"
Linebreak - "Evaporation"
No Tell Motel - "Directions to my House," "In Europe Everything's Different," "Lucid," "Robots," "This Cat, That Cat"
Pebble Lake Review - "Another Prayer"
Poetry - "The Brother Swimming Beneath Me"
Qarrtsiluni - "Robin Egg Blue"
Rattle - "Maps"
Six Sentences - "Behind"
Slipstream - "Bad Birthday"
Softblow - "Armless Iraqi Boy Bears No Grudges for U.S. Bombing," "Blood Poisoning," "Oysters," "Why I Can't Write a Paris Poem"

A selection from "Maier," originally titled "Peripheral," first appeared in the anthology *The Musculature Of Small Birds* (Shadowbox Press, 2007).

"Moving Past" also appeared in the chapbook *Trees are the Slowest Rivers* (Sarasota Poetry Theater Press, 1999)

i : Narrowly Missing the Moon

Another Prayer

Dear religion, there is no afterlife.
I hope you don't mind me saying this.

When you say *heaven on earth*
I think: the *dead read minds.*

When you think *dust to dust*
I say: *this body is a riverbed.*

Will the congregation please
recite what this wall of stained glass

is trying to tell you? Dear Buddha,
I've been knocking from the inside.

Heaven is not an ecosystem.
When I dream my brother visits me

it is my brother looking at his reflection
through my eyes, my sleeping tongue.

When we die we turn inside out and call
this turning a tunnel made of light.

Maps

The other night I spaced a stop sign
and ran it 60mph and died
but didn't. What algebra is this?
The night a dusty chalkboard
erased with moonlight, my life hwy K,
hwy 51 N intersecting K in a near-perfect T,
the afterlife this narrowing gravel road beyond pavement
disappearing into endless juniper and birch.
It was very dark and the signs obscured.
By heavens no screaming headlights
T-boned me into oblivion. Instead
I kicked up a little dust on the other side,
turned the pines brake-light red
and spun around: *fuck!* The very next night
I witnessed two logging trucks
cross each other north/south like two vault doors
slicing closed the ghost path
I blindly whistled through. Now every night
I approach that frightened intersection
with full attention. Sometimes
I die. Sometimes I continue. But most times
it's too close to call, the stars
always rearranging their astrologies,
each cloud narrowly missing the moon.

Séance

The dead assemble to summon the living.
Most skeptical: those spirits still grieving.

Others yet adjusting to their compound sight.
Imagine even God got it wrong – no directions

in this language. How will they ever
reach us, their hands now made of light?

Dust gathers dust. Each night they whisper
our names in unison, praying we will wake.

Doors and Windows for a Room

We make doors and windows for a room;
But it is these empty spaces that make the room livable.

– Lao Tzu

The point where light ends and all shadows begin
is sometimes called the body, these borrowed shoes
anchoring earth to passing sky. Seven flowers
exhale root to crown, a river of stars breathe
through us, we say one thing but always reveal
another. Why deep inside the groin do two stones
throb like a neon red motel marquee, this salt thirst
only the moon waning just above the pines, so many
cars passing without exit? Start taking the body
away: these searching hands, this open mouth,
the white crescent scar where the tumor grew.
How many spirits uncoil from the spine like galaxies
whirlpooling endlessly upward? The mind figures
it strange, this *almost rising*, heart tugging
throat, one last shiver under skin. What
vast dizziness now wheels behind the eyes?
Whose subtle body still searches for its form?

Meat to Carry Our Minds

Start here: the end of your body.
Go anywhere. The next life wanders,

frame by frame our spirits slide. A story
about a train stop in a town near where

you were born. Some ground us, some
abandon, each designs its own resignations.

Body to body this narrative threads
character to plot to pen. And when one

finally finds you, greet again this first life,
the grateful one, and all those who love you

shall follow. But this is what heaven –
any one of us at once? Any one of us?

Wisconsin Triptych

- after 3 paintings by David Lenz

Thistles

Let's say Irv and Mercedes have loved each other
for over 40 years, standing here backlit together
near the end of their rutted dusty private drive.

What heaven is this they've planted, plow chains
creaking taut against stubborn boulder and deadfall oak?
Early morning sun ignites mist steaming up from valley

to sky. Their sleeping border collie's shadow
yawns. Irv's sharp shoulder eclipses half his wife's stature,
grey hair haloed white as the thistle crowns gone to seed

between the barbed wire fence and her gently crossed arms.

Sam and the Perfect World

Cowlick. Lens glare. OshKosh B'Gosh.
Portrait at nine. The perfect world

winds all the way down valley.
Even the barbed wire bends with it.

The tall grass rivers toward the river.
The far horizon traces a simple ellipse

before a wind smudges it with a thin finger.
A sundog swallows everything: the eye

plays beautiful tricks. Like what space remains
beyond a watercolor's spill, this perfect sky

is mostly white, not blue. The whole world
shifts. Sam leans into it, still squinting at you.

Cold Front

He's climbed the quarter mile
up the winding back
of this terminal moraine.
Croplan cap. Salt-crusted brim.
Third day unshaven sunken throat.
His soil-smeared pale cotton shirt
worn so thin we can make out
the dark story of his skin bleeding through.
Such distance between this rise
and the last two Holsteins grazing the bottomland –
hiding behind the corrugated concrete silo, his family's home
primed white as a mortgage envelope.
A cold front's shadow floods half the pasture,
though up here he stands face in full sun,
watching the late summer storm
sliding open its thundering barn doors.

Blood Poisoning

At four I nearly died after a minor dog bite. One incisor sank into my palm and punctured my lifeline. The gray death traced my veins up my left arm to my shoulder, inches from my heart. Two weeks in the hospital, a green ceramic planter on my nightstand embossed with a smiling clown clutching multicolor balloons. Flowers bloomed from his head. Downtown Milwaukee, 36 floors vaulted into the skyline. My older brother Mark was too young to visit, so my mom would walk me to the window and lift me up to search the distant sidewalk below where he and my dad were supposed to be waiting. This was my small death, one which would eventually swallow him entirely. I waved, though I never remember seeing them. They waved back, though the outside windows mirrored the sky.

Cicada

Your name :: *august nearly empty*

Your body :: *a searching throat*

Your song :: *a viola playing its bow*

Your memory :: *veined translucent wings*

Your distance :: *by earth or sky*

Your cycle :: *bury a child's body underground*

Lice

Alcohol-beaded black combs divide
our hair into freshly opened books,
latex gloves snapping powder, fingers
squeaking against scalp in search
for signs of nits laid deep at the roots.
Surviving clean the school nurses'
inspections, entire class dismissed,
Tom and I after school sharing
his rec room futon too close for boys
our age, an encyclopedia eclipsing
both our laps – what other lives
inhabit the body unnoticed, what small
secrets passed host to host? Half joke,
half shy bold gesture, Tom hooks a thumb
under his white elastic Adidas waistband
to inspect the trace of hair rivering down
from navel to *there*, blonde and thin
as the soft hair curving above his
curiously-blue eyes questioning mine.

First Queer Poem

Of course I shake all my martinis Sapphire,
appreciate art, MFA'd, these shoes international,
chocolate chaise zen-modern, whip-smart attire.
By necktie noose I am a creative professional.

By night I product my hair to a perfect mess,
unwind my tongue around velour conversations.
Oh, do stop. My mirror adores me when I undress,
big boy, abs groomed smooth to chiseled definition.

Eyes up here, buddy. Your future wife is watching.
No secret: married men sometimes rest-stop cruise,
flashing headlights like sad lost deep sea creatures.
I live on the surface. I'm for real: ask me anything.

How dramatic my coming out, tears blurring my eyes.
Father puts his fork down. My mother feigns surprise.

Oysters

In San Jose I am closer to the ocean
where I take a stool alone at the hotel bar,
order my martini and five shucked half-shells
across a bed of ice and pepper-sharp sea beans,
plump briny flesh glistening in blue-white
iridescent light. Outside the mirrored glass façade,
downtown hurries past, each soul tuned inward
toward their own distant voices. I welcome memory
into my mouth, salty sweet flesh I hold
for a moment against my tongue: the first
gentle figure in darkness who arched her back
to my curious blindness. Or later, the young men
who taught me how to softly open my mouth
for love. What small embarrassment to think this now
as Roberto clears my plate and pours my second drink,
how I long after dark to roam this distant city
searching for another skin to press into my own,
to pry my shyness open like a shell. How what we want
will always share the moon with the sea, each small desire
emptying into something curved and waiting to fill again.

Why I Can't Write a Paris Poem

-for Joel Brouwer

Because escargot drowns in garlic herb butter and *fumé blanc*
the night of my arrival. Because a suicide leapt under the metro
turning everyone around at Gare du Nord and still
I navigated your rented 4th-floor efficiency by instinct alone.
Because the Arts Board ladled cash onto something unfinished
and I trusted Hemingway's ghost in the Latin Quarter would
forgive me for never having read his work. Because
I was 26. Because our friendship began with fan mail.
Because you insisted jetlag is cured by ignoring
what country your body thinks it's in. Because your wife
was natively fluent. Because salt peanuts and beer and spiced olives:
mélange piquant dripping oil from a merchant cart along Rue Mouffetard.
Because you offered me a day writing in C.K. Williams' studio
but reconsidered turning over the keys. Because you were right
not to. Because drunk in Place Pigalle I stumbled into a parlor
and asked for a massage and she thought I meant with her mouth
Because your manuscript was centuries stronger. Because
Rilke's panther yet paces the Jardin des Plantes and
I posed in front of a sign heralding *Le Printemps des Poètes*,
thinking all of this my season. Because the eye loves to believe
in the color of things. Because every photo to uncoil
from my camera I developed black & white.

Information Age

Behind cat's eyes hide mirrors. At night, the reflection of torches burn inside them.

*

The cursor taps its thin impatient finger against snow.

*

A photographer in Spain invites me to compose captions for a documentary about the war, pressing the SEND key like a doorbell.

*

A webpage printed on paper. Hyperlinks underlined in blue. The proofer sharpens her pencil, reaches for the department dictionary.

*

The error message asks *Are you sure you want to proceed?* A red line questions if I've spelled my name correctly.

*

First the batteries in my desktop meditation fountain drain dead. Then the water settles into thin air. The Buddha figurine kneels in an empty basin.

*

My father posts another anonymous comment.

*

A hunter-orange rebar mast rises behind my rural mailstop. In winter, snowed over, plowed in, the black breadbox door freezes on its rusting hinge.

*

The Sunarban Swampland Tiger swims up to 2 miles a day. A diver captures how outstretched paws shape efficient paddles. The narrator explains how big cats swim the same way they walk, walk the way they swim, chins skimming water.

*

I mistakenly *Reply All* to the message questioning your absence.

*

A single wire connects us to the world. Stretching for miles to the horizon, a clear-cut swath of forest towering with crosses, thin black lines slack between.

Improvisation

Just how many solos does it take to track
one seamless session, smokin' bebop head,
analog console, channel gliders glowing red,
engineers staring through wide glass at the back
of a tenor player punched in and waiting his cue?
You'd never know it nowadays, it all sounds
so old school, so first take, just how many rounds
get erased for better phrases, this impromptu
jazz experiment overdub-recorded ten times
or more to cherry pick the best solo for final mix.
Cans cranked, I love to listen past the studio tricks
and catch a hint of any discarded ghost line
mistakenly laid down when a mic bleeds through.
First thought, best thought? Cue take two.

"Armless Iraqi Boy Bears No Grudges for U.S. Bombing"

Doctors hope to fit him with rotating wrists and electrical hands that will allow him to do things like hold a book and turn the pages.

– Reuters, August 11, 2003

We know it is difficult to look at
when parts of him are still missing.
It will take some time for his charred skin
to completely slough off. It will take longer
for his arm stumps to forget how to carry
and for the two ragged holes to close.
His condition is improving. We have replaced
his eyes with rubble, his ears with crosshairs,
his mouth a khaki radio. We know
it is difficult to look at. Through his translator
he tells us he's grateful. We've replaced
his hair with burning oil fields, his stomach
for expired reservist rations, his broken spine
with a chalk-blue contrail. This is
expensive business. We are lucky to have allies
who help us carry the bill. An armless torso
is difficult to look at. He bears no grudges.
We have replaced his hands with fire, his legs
with landing gear, his entire family with shrapnel.
His father, pregnant mother, brother, aunt, three cousins
could not be untangled from the smoking rebar
where we found him. His arms would not
let go. Through his translator he tells us
he is lucky to have been saved. He is only one
example. There are many more we must help.
We might never find the right words
to carry what we're trying to exactly say.

ii : Evaporation

. . . Nothing resembles anything
else, we want only
new ways to love
memory.

– Marea Gordett

Kodachrome Slides of My Father in Vietnam

19, svelte, sunburnt, shy,
fire-headed bean pole,
M-14 marksman cross
stabbed into his lapel.

*

Birthday Lottery, televised
draft. Strip naked. Pull
the pin. Take this mezuzah
with you. Bring it home.

*

Drunk, lying face up
on the floodlit runway
at night, cargo planes
climbing, dropping flares.

*

Leaning at the base gate
against a sign in three
languages - Thai, English,
French: *You are a guest here.*

*

Here is your letter from home.
Here is your newborn son.
Here is your security clearance.
Here is the scissored hole where his name ███████████

*

My father is drowning
in a rice paddy, swallowing
duckweed and mud.
The bullet hole in his windshield

resembles a glass spider,
jeep overturned, one wheel
spinning smoke. A crosshair
searches for survivors.

Mayfly

Lake fly hatching
dulls the evening air.
Two summers before
my brother's diagnosis.
Returning indoors
to his oddly lit room –
the light he left on
darkened by a swarm.

Robin Egg Blue

Thigh to thigh on the slip-covered couch,
your legs clamped closed like the ladder

I trespassed through the neighbor's yard
before detention dismissed you later home.

Robin's call two days absent from the clotted
roof gutter nest. I wanted to see how another life

begins. The TV hisses between channels.
Your faded Levis I'd soon fill out myself.

Cool corrugated grip of the tallest rung turning
awkward as a zipper's deliberate downward cleaving.

Two pale blue eggs: the heavy leaf-litter must
of something abandoned. I wanted to be shown

what my body would become. Such slight
pressure, this fingernail digging in. The first egg

gives easily, thumb shattering through.
Should I say you taught me this? To take you

in my mouth and let you grow there? How
suddenly an afternoon changes light. Your knee

floors hard against belt buckle. The second egg
opens across the driveway's gritty tongue.

I see your skin has broken – a crescent impression
welling the blood-purple half-circle of some poor

embryo, only three exposed heartbeats remain.
The TV focuses its dimming pinpoint eye

as we empty the living room. Between two
fragile halves: that slick amber yolk relaxing

outward, darkening the sparkling gravel.

Maier

Mark, I write
your Hebrew name, *Maier,*

and press it into the open palm
of the newborn cousin who inherits

your name, whose soft eyes
already search to understand you,

the rich syllables of your story
curving in the air between us –

Mark,
           Maier,

please watch
and give him footsteps.

*

Which face should I remember?
The doctor says *blood brothers*, suggests
I imagine my brother's cancer as weeds
strangling a garden: to kill what's invasive

we have to purge the soil – radiation, chemo,
my younger marrow the new seeds, the new
seeds, my AB+ replacing his B+
like forget-me-nots.

                    O Brother of fluorescent light
and morphine nausea, your isolation suite
is waiting. The nurse will return shortly
to draw more blood. Each thin needle
whispering: *harvest, transplant, rejection . . .*

*

One of my earliest memories is waking up on my Grandma's couch with fever, parents laughing in the other room, my older brother Mark playing on the floor in front of the TV with little green army men. The television was an old fishbowl screen from the early '60s, fat channel knobs, and whatever program he was watching flickered grey and corduroy.

I stared at my brother, head titled, humming, pushing a toy tank around. Over his head, the news, and the anchorman had one of those signal ghosts sitting next to him which swam in and out of clarity (every person on my Grandma's old TV had a ghost standing or sitting or lighting a cigarette beside them). Looking away from the screen, my head swam, throbbing.

Some glasses clinked in the dining room. Scratching the wool blanket over my chest, I watched my brother sitting bent-kneed on the floor, white athletic socks ringed sky blue on the ankles, and I had trouble focusing: he split, wavering ghost sliding like a transparency to the right, hovering, then back, before I closed my eyes and fell asleep again.

*

Mark stands at the mirror,
blue kepah set on his head
like a tiny map of the world.
I can't tie a double Windsor
but my brother's learning,
ten, halfway through his life.
An hour before synagogue.
I'm sorry for starting that day,
sorry for the white sheet
of his bare chest. I can't tie

so I'm watching him dress,
each button a deliberate process,
me moving from the doorway
to the mirror, drawing a silk tie
through my fingers again
and again. I'm sorry
for his brown hair, bowl cut,
sorry for the fingers working
his collar, twist and gentle tug,
the tilt of his head, open mouthed.
I memorized this careful loop
and threading of fabric, the musk
of English Leather, dark suit coat
sharpening his shoulders, the fine
hairs on his cheek. Both our faces
in the mirror now, my clumsy hands
copying his. I'm sorry for all of this
now: his childlike humming, bright
blue eyes, the small knot, practiced
and taut, rising toward his throat.

*

five bleached oxfords
billow on the line

shoulders rigid
        with plastic hanger

sleeves lifting
            like sails

standing out here late
        evening   how many

days spent sorting
        what of his fits

or does not
        fit me

a wind picks up
        and for a moment

reaching for the line
                the whole yard –

*

Bald, no eyebrows,
TV muted in the isolation room,
post transplant, whirring IV,
brothers of the same flickering bulb.

To make your blood whole again
I went under for hours in a thin paper gown.
They drew the seeds of your new blood
by hammering hollow nails through skin
to reach the dark marrow inside my bones.

Tonight the nurse suspends this harvest
high above on a blunt hook between us
in a round, clear pouch:

a red moon draining into your pale arm.

*

As Mark turned eighteen, his body suddenly started shutting
down. He grew tired, sleeping in, missing work. A simple sore
throat took hold, his breath chronically sour enough for me to
turn my head away each time we talked.

Blood, always, in the white sink basin each time he'd brush
his teeth and spit. These were the first clues hissing *Leukemia,*
stunted blood cells suddenly roaming unkind, choking out
platelet and T-cell.

So then the months of chemotherapy, but still the doctors
frowned over each lab result.

Resistant, they said. *Acute.*

*

Thorn bushes surround
our great oak. All summer

the sprinkler waves its dull wet hand,
two brothers shirtless, laughing.

Squirrel's nest above, newborns
dark gray in thin damp fur.

Once a friend told me of a cemetery tree
growing through a child's grave.

The sprinkler waves. Believe this:
in the first bare weeks of October

I'd find, tangled among the thorn bushes,
their punctured, fallen bodies. Somewhere

I read the word squirrel is born
from *shadow* and *tail*. Mark

bloodies his knee. The small bones
of a child's hand rising from the earth.

*

Less than three years after the successful transplant, Mark
died with my blood in his veins. The immunosuppressants to
prevent his body from rejecting my blood let a simple knee
abrasion bloom into terminal infection.

*

Huge, silent, moving
away, face which will not turn,
wavering in the slow pulse of the last
minute, cardiac monitor keening,
your mouth slacked open. Once,

your doctor asked me to imagine you
a garden. Instead I see your eyes
lowering as you thread your body
out your bedroom window school nights
silent as smoke. Or your hazy, sunken eyes
returning before dawn, surprised by
a door suddenly opening.

*

We know the dead
through the eyes of birds.
You must turn your sight
almost completely away

to see them most clearly.
I want to call them *peripheral*.

Sly. *Floaters inside the eye.*
And the living? How quietly

a plane passes overhead –

The Brother Swimming Beneath Me

is not dead yet, though the water
he moves through is green and dark,
and the shadow from the bluff presses down
like a hand over us both, and the eelgrass
must catch lightly against his legs, must bend
with his passing and lengthen, and stay,
this boy who is not dead yet gliding flesh tone
and wavering hair past, though I want to say
I'm floating in an oar boat and his face is hidden
or blurry, I can see him again and again,
all snorkel and fin and dolphin kick, reaching forward
through handfuls of wavering light;
and ten years before his death his blood is still whole
and smooth through his veins – no – I mean to say
my brother swimming beneath me isn't only that day
on the lake, I'm saying this now because we live
on water and the dead move through us
and we bend with their passing, and lengthen, and stay;
I can feel the dull pull of the oars as I follow him
back to shore, tracing a rise of air through water
meeting air, his hands reaching forward
as the shadow from the cliff darkens us both
and he glides through it into the smell of wood smoke;
my shoulders work-sore and that first weight in my chest
I would later call grief; while now I turn the words
bowline, half hitch, cat's paw over and over again in my hands,
I should say I'm tying this thin rope to splintered wood,
I'm careful and maybe too slow or didn't pay attention
when my brother showed me this because
he's already just footfalls on the pier and fading now,
the note of each board heavy and muted, me floating
there on the water, stepping out onto the pier, this pull,
this weight, my brother's footsteps small wet splashes
on the woodgrain already soaking through, shrinking and gone
before he reaches the top of the stair – I have to say
his footprints disappear before I can put down my own
though I can still hear him rising, rising.

Moving Past

All morning the light streams past, glancing off pop cans
in the overstuffed garbage bin, rusted chain link hanging slack
between aluminum posts along the walk and a young woman
moving past in a V-neck tee, silver crucifix sparking
against that bare space – what arrives misses us
and comes back

*

                         disguised as color, cardinal in winter shrub,
blue bottle perched on the curb as if someone said *here, wait,*
I forgot something. Comes back disguised as song wavering
from a slowly passing car, windows down (and this the shocking
first weather of Reggae and tank tops), disguised as this street
pouring its flood of traffic into parking structure and tow-away zone.
                                           Can what arrives

*

be discerned from what's remembered?
An old man in the bookstore smells
like green onions – not his breath, not sour:
dirt fresh. And here in the photography aisle
I step through him into the past,
shirtless scuffle along the far bank
of Green Lake, brother pressing
my face into the mud, a stand
of short onion grass.

                         He is looking at a book
on gardens, and when I have to excuse myself
behind him, he leans into the tall shelves,
clutching the open pages to his chest
as if trying to keep a seagull
from flying away. Moving past,
his voice is a hand-cranked gramophone
winding down.

*

         Memory might be thin
as this wire connecting a man's brain to a monitor,
the mind's shape in colored cross-sections, thermal photos of an island
seen by satellite: he is sitting in a lab, tangle of electrodes
webbing his forehead and shoulders. He's holding a lukewarm apple
with two hands, while behind the mirror

                             technicians nod
and draw circles around the part of his mind actually seeing
apple, those lobes glowing: *yes, apple.*

But then they take the fruit away,
blindfold him.
               They want to learn
what part of the mind remembers.
Ask him to concentrate:

                       apple.

*

Apple. What arrives filters through this web
of branches lining the street, the hundred eye-
glass lenses of pedestrians, filters through
inward rivers of nerve and synapse spark, wavering echo
of your brother's name off the high cliff (does the ear know
whether it's listening or remembering?), filters
through the gills of memory fanning its fins in dark water.

You begin to think there never was the lake
or rented cottage, the sunburned walks
to the marina for crawlers. There never was
onion grass haunting the shore or a broken-down shack
you'd skinny away to. It was summer

*

                      then. All day the sun
pressed its back against faded wood. Believe me:
you could go there, even now – this late
in the evening – open your palms
and still feel
           where his body leaned.

Evaporation

My dropout brother swears a mouthful of freon
at the pressure gauge factory – his station
calibrated fittings for water mains, rescue
squads, crimson ladder trucks. Freon line
obstructed, he lifts the cool siphon to his mouth.
What were you thinking? Seventeen, saving
for his first kick-ass import MGB. Shift
supervisor scoffing, Skoal-yellow teeth:
Dumbass move, Goodman. He cuts a corner
and splices his blood in two. Grief begins with how,
not why. First week in oncology Mark confides in mom:
*Before I could do anything, it just evaporated
in my mouth. It was there, and then it was gone.*
I wasn't there, sawdust concrete floor,
siphon rising to his lips. He came home
ghost-faced, went to bed. Dreamt he
swallowed sky until his blood turned
to wind. Shift supervisor retelling the story
at home over dinner, mouth spitting peas,
fork in his piggy fist. Mark cuts a corner
and swallows glass, his blood squeezed
thin as a microscope slide. *It was there, then
it was gone.* Grief begins with a story
I'm not sure how to tell. Eighteen years
after his funeral mom confides to us
a new religion that almost explains
everything. *Before I could do anything,
it just evaporated in my mouth.* That night
I came home ghost-faced, went to bed.
Dreamt us careening his convertible up Holy Hill,
switchback wooded moraines, top down
as it starts to drizzle. Dear dropout sick
of school, your blood swallows wind. Grief
begins with every story I try to tell. I wasn't there,
your hair thinning to nothing. My mouth burns cold.
Rain on the windshield disappearing fast as it falls.

iii : Spiral Course

[directions to my house]

Bail your first career. Slouch stoned and indignant in your boss's corner office as he scuttles the company to outside interests. Take a hard left where your 20s burn two black lines into the blooming median. Here, think of my hand as a map. Travel all day north until you've climbed to the fingertips of Wisconsin. Six lanes narrow to four, two, gravel, pinecones. I'll glowstick the mailbox for ya. I've left the doors unlocked.

[this cat, that cat]

Outside there's nothing but a crow's feather twitching in the rain gauge. Inside the windows unpack their thin white shirts. She clings to his cologne like the damp black hair stringing her bare shoulders. This cat, that cat. A ceiling fan debates the air. She shares his button-down, boils oolong in an antique shop kettle. A spoon is not a mirror. This cat, that cat. Her Nokia says nothing. His tiny plane pierces a hole in a distant cloud.

[lucid]

He decided sleep wasn't good enough. He lined the inside of his skull with black velvet, turned the music down low. The whiskey helped too. He wrote elaborate dream vignettes with dialogue and dramatic tension and hidden meanings, submitting them to a black mailbox at the end of a dead end street. His hand disappears inside. Then arm, torso, legs, etc. The moon above as small as the dim LED indicating something's ON, or OFF.

[robots]

Build me a robot to clean the litterbox. One who butters toast, draws baths, archives my rare music library. Build me a robot that wants me to build him another robot and so on. Fill my house with enough machines to erase any clue I really live here. I don't like robots who look like me: fleshmatic skin, one raised eyebrow, fingertips articulate enough to vase an orchid. Build me a robot I can wear like a diver's suit. Bring me one who'll listen.

[science fiction]

For this role I learned to play the Theremin. The plot unfolds: after the spaceship tears through the water tower all the cows' milk turns to ash. At first, we welcome them in the cool shaded corn rows. Then green army men descend in their own shiny aircraft. Before our pets go missing, before our children turn against us, the general radios the president. I play the scientist who insists they're more like us than anyone might imagine.

[recipe]

Muddle your plans in a mortar. Marinade your house in balsamic vinegar, dijon, szechuan pepper & salt. Smash your leased vehicle with the flat side of your knife to release its essential oils. Now pick a wine: only cook with what you'd sip. Let the invitations rise on the countertop before baking them off G.B.D. Deglaze your marriage to a delicate simmer. A bay leaf helps. Thyme. Reduce your life by half until it coats the back of a spoon.

[in europe everything's different]

Men kissing men, children drinking wine, dinner past 11, money more coins than not. Women? Fuzzy pits, Birkenstock calves, coffee table photo albums documenting summer-long topless excursions to the beach. Pass the bread, pass the red, teach me *boules* in the Roman courtyard after dark. *Comme ci comme ça,* as they say. Sell me postcards and collectable brass landmark miniatures. Show me on this map where it says *You Are Here.*

[cover]

He wanted to sing it the way the radio sang it: invisible, tenuous,
static snowing between stations. He wanted to sing it how
the distant towers on the hill disappeared each night, only
two sad red beacons left signaling the empty dark. Not how
someone in love would sing it. Not how someone wanting
love would. Maybe he'd sing it from inside a tern or gull.
Maybe he'd turn his lungs to glass. Maybe he'd sing it solo in
a windowless room.

[bad birthday]

What a day to declare the world an ingrown hair, pinched nerve, bleeding ulcer. Lesson learned: insincere service at celebrations antagonizes anniversaries. Sharpie a red slash through this date, bite your cheek, seal the belated singing card with scented beeswax. Let the final guest finish the fancy nut mix. A week after the party and still the foil balloons wander around the apartment beating their heads along the stucco ceiling.

[behind]

Behind the house we ungrounded lightning rods where copper wires plunged deep into clay. Shot squirrels with pellet pistols hiding cool CO2 cartridges in their grips. Missed most times. Behind that tree the neighbor girl's swimsuit grew elastic. Take the crucifix off the rec room wall and hide his broken arms behind the couch. Behind her eyes question marks curl into hooks. It begins to thunder. Behind my brother I turn to shadow.

[superstitions]

Whistle at night? Invite home ghosts. Catch a falling crow's feather and your sister grows blind. When a light bulb sparks and hisses, recite your brother's name. See an owl perched in an old oak once: good luck. Twice, bad omen. Splash your door with lamb's blood. Toss the redhead down the well. Stack stones where the journey starts so your spirit knows where to return. Pour a glass of Manischewitz for Elijah, open the front door, wait.

[hebrew school]

Bar Mitzvah scrapped by 4th grade. Teach me your ancient
tongue, but only as symbol to sound. Read me, don't speak
me. Synagogue recess: bitter kosher chocolate, ghosts in the
cloakroom claiming their black wool overcoats. Shape my
embrasure to your instrument. Call me Ze'ev or Leo or Vulf.
A language thread through with mathematics. Every Saturday
Moses eclipsed the classroom wall, wind in hair, pointing
vaguely upward.

[drift]

He took so many pills he started hearing voices. He stopped
sleeping. The cats grew thin and yowled and shat in the wilted
planters. At work he stared down the glazed computer, drafting
memos and tearing them up unread. He forgot about his lover
ten years. His dead brother finally slipped his mind. He kept it
together. The fish turned belly up. The phone grew suspicious
and oddly distant. His eyes cowered in their purple caves.

[scars]

The glossy spooned out quarter on my calf where a tumor
anointed my childhood. Or here, where a tooth sunk in. A
constellation of white stars mapping the small of my back.
The girl who cuts herself pulls her sleeves down. In my knee
the shrapnel that pierced my father's 20s. This scar is my
covenant with God. On TV the mystic blossoms red flowers
from her palms, recites the rosary, opens her blouse to reveal
a blood-seared cross.

[leukemia]

Too much blood for one boy's body. Marrow gone stuttering wrong. Learn to understand what language the microscope sees. *You can have everything.* Take this heart-bound catheter, this twitching foot, this bedpan slick with phlegm. Selfish blood. Blood thin as transparent red gauze. Teach me your language, goddamn foreigner. After the diagnosis, I looked you up. I stood in a room, opened a book, introduced my life to yours.

[by definition]

To move by elastic force. Something that obscures. Concerned with remote things. An issue of water from the earth. To move in a circular or spiral course. To keep vigil as a devotional exercise. A glazed structure above an opening in a roof for light. The part by which an object is attached to another. An immaterial essence, animating principle, actuating cause. An object that makes an electrical connection with the earth.

[love letter]

You never sing along anymore when I belt out show tunes in the living room or steady your blocking when I leap into your arms from atop the creaking armoire. Dearest dear, the cats demand an encore. This take, pretend not to notice I'm not wearing any knickers. And *action!* The olives in my martini lean forward. You just glare at me like a lost line. Haven't we been rehearsing this goddamn performance upwards of fifteen years now?

[how was your weekend?]

Three lesbians and a pack of dogs. One bit me (the dogs).
There was Disaronno, a joint, and occasional robot dancing
involved. Later, there were two middle-aged women wedgie
wrestling between the couch and TV. I sang "Come Sail Away"
on a Casio keyboard to a samba rhythm preset. At one point
there were jazz hands. They were mine. I visited my friends in
a city I used to live in. I drove a great distance to get back.

[famous last words]

I don't want to die with a quote bit under my tongue. I don't want my last words to be *I love you* or a distant hug goodbye. Give me the courage to write my last line in time to revise it. The last thing I said to my brother's body was an on-the-spot lie. Edison whispered: *It's very beautiful over there.* That's good. Let my last words be a window or climax of a beautiful story. Oscar Wilde's last breath: *Either those curtains go or I do!*

[past lives]

Redhead suicide, scarlet fever, holocaust, third rail, stillborn.
Best not to blame past lives for migraines, luck, regret, or
déjà vu. Haifa. Sapporo. Luxembourg. Eden. Each life learns
to outlive the last. Eat rich meals, fuck, haunt museums,
Eurorail every hostel from Amsterdam to Zagreb. Chalk a
line around your silhouette near the fountain. Pray your
children may survive you. Dear mystery: are you the outline,
shadow, earth or sun?